Homeowner's Insurance Handbook

Protecting Your Biggest Investment

Cheryl Waller, MBA

ISBN: 9798396490123

LEGAL DISCLAIMER: This publication is designed to provide accurate and authoritative information in regard to the subject matter covered. The publisher is not engaged in rendering legal, accounting, or other professional services. If legal advice or other expert assistance is required, the services of a competent professional should be sought.

TABLE OF CONTENTS

INTRODUCTION TO HOMEOWNER'S INSURANCE: YOUR FIRST LINE OF DEFENSE

Your home is more than just a roof over your head. It's a sanctuary, a haven where you and your loved ones create lasting memories. It's also likely to be your most valuable financial investment. Protecting it should therefore be a top priority, and this is where homeowner's insurance comes into play.

The concept of homeowner's insurance can be traced back to the Great Fire of London in 1666. This devastating event, which razed more than 13,000 houses, served as a brutal reminder of the potential financial losses homeowners could face. Over the centuries, the practice has evolved, offering homeowners a safety net to protect their precious abode and its contents from unforeseen events or perils.

At its core, homeowner's insurance is a contract between you and the insurance company. It stipulates that in exchange for your payment of a premium, the insurance company agrees to pay for certain types of damage to your property and personal possessions. It also provides liability coverage in case someone gets injured on your property and decides to sue.

Why Do You Need Homeowner's Insurance?

Let's start by addressing the most fundamental question: Why do you need homeowner's insurance? Firstly, it's about financial protection. Imagine a scenario where your house is damaged by a fire, storm, or burglary. Without insurance, the cost of rebuilding, repairing, or replacing your possessions would come out of your pocket. An insurance policy cushions you against such potentially crippling financial hits.

Secondly, if you have a mortgage on your home, your lender will typically require you to have homeowner's insurance. They want to ensure their investment is protected. In fact, your monthly mortgage payment likely includes an escrow payment that goes toward your homeowner's insurance premium.

Finally, homeowner's insurance provides liability coverage. If someone is injured on your property and decides to sue, your homeowner's insurance could help cover the cost of legal fees and any potential settlements. This is a significant benefit, as legal expenses can be exorbitantly high and can jeopardize your financial stability.

The Four Components of a Standard Homeowner's Insurance Policy

A standard homeowner's insurance policy generally comprises four key components:

- Dwelling Coverage: This pays for damage to the house itself and anything attached to it, such as a garage. It's crucial to have enough dwelling coverage to rebuild your home in case of total loss.

- Personal Property Coverage: This protects your belongings within the home, such as furniture, clothing, and electronics. If they're stolen or damaged by a covered peril, you can file a claim to get them replaced or repaired.

- Liability Coverage: This protects you if someone outside your household gets injured on your property and you're found legally responsible. It also covers damage you, your family members, or your pets may cause to other people's property.

- Additional Living Expenses (ALE) Coverage: If your home is uninhabitable after a disaster, ALE coverage helps pay for temporary housing and living expenses while your home is being repaired or rebuilt.

Adjusting Your Policy to Your Needs

A homeowner's insurance policy is not a one-size-fits-all solution. Different homeowners have different insurance needs based on factors such as the type of home they own, its location, its age, and the value of their belongings.

For example, if you own expensive jewelry, original artwork, or high-end electronics, you might need to purchase additional personal property coverage. If your home is located in an area prone to floods or earthquakes, you might need to buy separate policies for these perils, as they are often not covered under standard homeowner's insurance. In some cases, older homes may require additional coverage due to increased risks associated with outdated electrical or plumbing systems.

Thus, it's crucial to carefully review and understand your policy, including its limits and exclusions. It's equally important to revisit your insurance needs annually or whenever significant life changes occur, such as a home renovation, the purchase of valuable items, or a change in your home's occupancy.

Choosing the Right Deductible

A significant aspect of homeowner's insurance that you'll need to decide upon is your deductible, which is the amount you'll have to pay out of pocket before your insurance coverage kicks in.

Typically, the higher your deductible, the lower your premium. It might be tempting to choose a high deductible to save on your monthly payments, but it's crucial to consider whether you would be able to afford the out-of-pocket costs if disaster strikes. A lower deductible, while resulting in a higher premium, can offer greater peace of mind knowing you won't be faced with unmanageable costs following an unexpected event.

Benefit of Home Maintenance

An often overlooked aspect of homeowner's insurance is the importance of regular home maintenance. Keeping your home in good repair can prevent many common perils that homeowners face. For instance, routinely cleaning your gutters can prevent water damage, while regular checks on your home's electrical system can prevent fires.

Importantly, regular maintenance can also make the claims process smoother. Insurance companies may deny claims if they find that negligence or poor maintenance has contributed to the damage.

Rising to the Challenge

Understanding and managing homeowner's insurance can feel like an intimidating task, but it is a necessary part of protecting your most significant investment. With a clear grasp of the basics, you can navigate the ins and outs of homeowner's insurance confidently.

As we journey through this book, we'll delve into the intricacies of homeowner's insurance, from understanding the terms and conditions of your policy, assessing the value of your home and possessions, and comparing different types of policies, to the claims process, and much more. Our aim is to arm you with the knowledge and insights needed to make informed decisions about your homeowner's insurance.

Indeed, homeowner's insurance is your first line of defense in safeguarding your home. It's about more than just satisfying your mortgage lender's requirements - it's about protecting your sanctuary, your memories, and your financial future. In the chapters that follow, we will equip you with the knowledge and tools to do just that, ensuring that you can rest easy knowing that your home is well protected.

Understanding Covered Perils

Not all types of damage are covered under a standard homeowner's insurance policy. Covered perils typically include events like fire, windstorms, hail, lightning, theft, vandalism, and explosions. However, some major disasters like floods and earthquakes are often excluded and require separate policies.

Homeowner's insurance is more than just a mandatory requirement by your mortgage lender. It's your first line of defense against a variety of potential financial disasters that could result from damage to your home or personal liability claims. It's crucial to thoroughly understand your policy and ensure it adequately covers your home and possessions.

UNDERSTANDING YOUR HOME'S VALUE: KEY FACTORS AND ASSESSMENT

One of the foundational aspects of protecting your home through insurance is understanding its value. In the world of insurance, it's not about the market value of your home, but the replacement cost – the amount required to rebuild or repair your home in the event of a disaster. Let's delve deeper into how to assess this critical element.

Defining Home Value

When it comes to home insurance, the value of your home isn't measured by its selling price, its market value, or even its tax-assessed value. Instead, insurers use a concept called the "replacement cost". This term refers to the amount of money it would take to replace your home from the ground up at current material and labor prices, not factoring in depreciation. Replacement cost is critical for determining how much dwelling coverage you should have in your homeowner's insurance policy.

Factors That Influence Your Home's Value

A multitude of factors can influence the replacement cost of your home, including:

- Size and Structure: Larger homes typically cost more to replace. The same goes for homes with more complex structures, such as those with multiple stories, unusual layouts, or specialized design features.

- Construction Materials: Homes built with high-end, expensive materials cost more to replace than those built with standard materials. Specialized or custom materials can further increase the replacement cost.

- Local Construction Costs: The cost of labor and materials in your local area will significantly influence your home's replacement cost. These costs can vary considerably from one region to another.

- Home Improvements: Major improvements or renovations can increase your home's replacement cost. For instance, if you've added an extension, upgraded your kitchen, or renovated your bathroom, you should reevaluate your replacement cost.

- Special Features: Unique features like custom-built-ins, fireplaces, outdoor living spaces, and luxury fittings can add to the replacement cost.

Assessing Your Home's Value

Understanding your home's value for insurance purposes can be a complex process. It's often recommended to hire a professional home replacement cost estimator, who can provide a detailed evaluation of your home's features and give you a more accurate figure for its replacement cost. Many insurance companies offer this service for free or a small fee.

However, if you'd like to do an initial estimation yourself, you can follow these steps:

- Calculate the Building Size: Start by determining the total square footage of your home. Then consider the number of rooms, bathrooms, and any additional structures like garages or sheds.

- Identify Materials and Special Features: Take inventory of the materials used in your home, both inside and out. Note any high-end finishes or special features. Remember to include elements like roofing, flooring, kitchen and bathroom fittings, and other permanent fixtures.

- Check Local Construction Costs: Research the average cost per square foot to build a home in your local area. Construction companies or a quick online search can provide this information.

- Add It Up: Multiply the total square footage of your home by the local construction cost per square foot. Add any additional costs for special features or high-end materials. The result should give you a rough estimate of your home's replacement cost.

Keep in mind that this is a simplified method, and it may not account for all factors affecting your home's replacement cost. Always consult with a professional or your insurance agent for a more accurate assessment.

Revisiting Your Home's Value

Evaluating your home's replacement cost isn't a one-time process. It's essential to reassess this value every few years or whenever significant changes to your home occur. For example, if you've completed a major renovation or added a new addition, these changes could considerably increase the replacement cost of your home. Similarly, fluctuations in local construction costs can also affect the replacement cost value over time.

Additionally, market inflation can cause both construction costs and home values to increase. Even without significant renovations, the replacement cost of your home could rise over time due to inflation. To account for this, some insurance companies offer inflation protection coverage, which automatically adjusts your coverage limit each year to account for inflation.

Understanding Co-Insurance Clauses

A key insurance concept related to replacement cost is the co-insurance clause. This clause, found in many insurance policies, stipulates that you must insure your home for a certain percentage (usually around 80%) of its replacement cost.

If you fail to do so and suffer a loss, you may be penalized and receive less compensation than you expect. The co-insurance penalty could leave you with a significant out-of-pocket expense in the event of a claim, even if it's for less than the total loss of your home.

For example, if your home's replacement cost is $500,000, and your insurance policy has an 80% co-insurance clause, you must have at least $400,000 in coverage. If you're only insured for $300,000, you may be penalized and receive less compensation for your loss.

To avoid such a situation, it's crucial to maintain an up-to-date assessment of your home's replacement cost and to ensure that your coverage limits meet the requirements of your policy's co-insurance clause.

Conclusion

Understanding your home's value is a fundamental step in securing adequate home insurance coverage. It's about more than just knowing how much you could sell your house for in today's market. It's about understanding the intricacies of replacement cost and the many factors that can influence it.

Your home's replacement cost forms the basis of your dwelling coverage limit, which is a crucial component of your homeowner's insurance policy. An accurate assessment of this value ensures that you're adequately protected in the event of a disaster. Moreover, understanding and maintaining an accurate replacement cost can help you avoid penalties under your policy's co-insurance clause, protecting your financial stability in the event of a claim.

In the upcoming chapters, we will further explore the different components of a home insurance policy, including dwelling coverage, personal property coverage, and liability coverage, as well as additional living expenses coverage. With a comprehensive understanding of your home's value, you'll be well-equipped to navigate these topics and to tailor your insurance coverage to your unique needs. It's a crucial step in safeguarding your biggest investment – your home.

TYPES OF HOME INSURANCE POLICIES: A COMPARATIVE STUDY

Navigating the world of homeowner's insurance can feel overwhelming due to the wide array of insurance policies available. Each policy type offers different coverage levels, making it essential to understand these distinctions to ensure your home and belongings are adequately protected. In this chapter, we will provide a comparative study of the most common types of home insurance policies.

Common Home Insurance Policy Types

Insurance policies in the United States are typically standardized and named using an HO (Homeowners) system. Here are the most commonly used policy types:

- HO-1: Basic Form Homeowner Policy: An HO-1 policy offers the least amount of coverage among homeowner's insurance policies. It covers your dwelling and personal property against a limited number of perils, typically including fire or smoke, explosions, lightning, hail and windstorms, theft, vandalism, damage from vehicles, and volcanic eruption. However, due to its limited coverage, many insurers no longer offer this policy type.

- HO-2: Broad Form Homeowner Policy: HO-2 policies provide more comprehensive coverage than HO-1 policies. They cover your home and personal property against 16 named perils, including all those covered by an HO-1 policy, plus damage caused by falling objects, weight of ice, snow or sleet, freezing of household systems, accidental discharge or overflow of water or steam, and sudden and accidental tearing apart, cracking, burning, or bulging of pipes and other household systems.

- HO-3: Special Form Homeowner Policy: This is the most common type of homeowner's insurance policy. HO-3 policies offer "open peril" coverage for your home, meaning they cover all risks of physical loss to your dwelling except those specifically excluded in the policy. Personal property, however, is still covered on a "named peril" basis, similar to an HO-2 policy.

- HO-5: Comprehensive Form Homeowner Policy: HO-5 policies provide the most extensive coverage. Like an HO-3 policy, an HO-5 policy provides open peril coverage for your dwelling. However, it also extends this open peril coverage to your personal property, making it a more comprehensive option.

- HO-6: Condo Insurance: If you own a condominium, an HO-6 policy is what you need. It covers personal property, liability, and improvements to the unit you own and reside in.

- HO-8: Older Home Insurance: HO-8 policies are designed for older homes that would be costly to repair or replace to their original condition due to the use of obsolete or custom materials and techniques. Instead of replacement cost coverage, these policies typically provide modified replacement cost or actual cash value coverage, which accounts for depreciation.

Choosing the Right Policy

Selecting the right homeowner's insurance policy requires careful consideration of your needs and circumstances. Here are some factors to consider:

- Coverage Needs: Begin by determining your coverage needs. Consider the replacement cost of your home and the value of your personal property. You should also consider your liability risks.

- Risk Tolerance: Evaluate your risk tolerance. Can you afford a higher deductible for lower premiums? How much out-of-pocket cost could you handle in the event of a loss?

- Policy Exclusions: Review the exclusions in each policy type. Are there risks that aren't covered that you want coverage for? If so, you might need to purchase additional coverage or a different type of policy.

- Cost: Consider the cost of each policy type. While an HO-5 policy offers the most coverage, it's also likely to be the most expensive. Can you afford the higher premiums for the added coverage, or would a lower-cost policy be more suitable for your budget?

Endorsements and Floaters

If you find that none of the standard homeowner's insurance policy types fully meet your needs, consider endorsements and floaters. These are additions or amendments to your insurance policy that can provide coverage for perils, properties, or situations not covered by your standard policy.

Endorsements can cover a wide range of risks. For example, you can add an endorsement for water backup coverage, which covers damage caused by water backing up through your drains or sewer, a peril that's typically excluded from standard policies.

Floaters or riders are usually used to cover high-value items, like jewelry or fine art, beyond the coverage limits of your standard policy. If you own such items, consider adding a floater to ensure they're fully protected.

Renters and Landlord Insurance

While this chapter mainly focuses on homeowners, it's worth noting the existence of other forms of home insurance. If you're a renter, a Renters Insurance policy (HO-4) can cover your personal property, liability, and additional living expenses if a covered peril makes your rental unit uninhabitable.

If you're a landlord, Landlord Insurance (often called Dwelling Fire policy or DP) can cover the dwelling, other structures, loss of rental income, and liability. This type of policy is essential if you rent out a property, as standard homeowner's policies may not provide coverage in this situation.

Conclusion

Understanding the different types of homeowner's insurance policies is key to selecting the right coverage for your needs. Each policy type offers a different level and scope of coverage, with its unique advantages and drawbacks.

Consider your individual circumstances, your home, your personal property, and your risk tolerance when choosing a policy. Remember, the goal of homeowner's insurance is to provide financial protection and peace of mind. The right policy for you is the one that best fulfills this goal, given your unique situation and needs.

In the chapters to come, we will delve deeper into the individual components of a homeowner's insurance policy, including dwelling coverage, other structures coverage, personal property coverage, liability coverage, and additional living expenses coverage. With a comprehensive understanding of the different types of home insurance policies, you'll be well-equipped to understand these topics and to tailor your insurance coverage to your unique needs. It's a crucial step in safeguarding your biggest investment – your home.

COVERAGE EXPLAINED: WHAT YOUR HOME INSURANCE POLICY SHOULD INCLUDE

Home insurance coverage is the bedrock of your financial protection as a homeowner. Knowing what your policy covers is essential to understanding the protection it provides and, just as importantly, what it does not cover. In this chapter, we will break down the main components of a standard homeowner's insurance policy.

The Anatomy of Home Insurance Coverage

Most home insurance policies contain six essential types of coverage:

- Dwelling Coverage
- Other Structures Coverage
- Personal Property Coverage
- Loss of Use or Additional Living Expenses Coverage
- Personal Liability Coverage
- Medical Payments to Others Coverage

Let's delve deeper into each of these to provide a comprehensive understanding of what your home insurance policy should include.

Dwelling Coverage

Dwelling coverage is the cornerstone of any home insurance policy. It provides coverage for the physical structure of your home – the walls, floors, ceilings, and any other part of the main building. It's designed to pay for repairs or reconstruction if your home is damaged or destroyed by a covered peril, such as fire, hail, or vandalism.

When setting your dwelling coverage limit, it's crucial to base it on the replacement cost of your home – the amount it would cost to rebuild your home using similar materials and construction methods. This is a key concept we explored in Chapter 2.

Other Structures Coverage

Other structures coverage protects structures on your property that are separate from your main house. This can include detached garages, sheds, fences, and even your driveway. Typically, other structures coverage is set as a percentage of your dwelling coverage, usually around 10%.

Personal Property Coverage

Personal property coverage protects your personal belongings, including furniture, clothing, electronics, and appliances, whether they're located in your home or temporarily outside your home. Like dwelling coverage, personal property coverage can pay to repair or replace your belongings if they're damaged or destroyed by a covered peril.

Most policies offer personal property coverage as a percentage of your dwelling coverage, usually between 50% to 70%. However, it's essential to note that certain types of high-value items, like jewelry or artwork, typically have lower coverage limits. If you own such items, consider purchasing additional coverage, such as a personal property endorsement or floater.

Loss of Use or Additional Living Expenses Coverage

If a covered peril makes your home uninhabitable, loss of use or additional living expenses (ALE) coverage can help cover the increased living costs you incur as a result. This can include hotel bills, restaurant meals, and other costs above and beyond your normal living expenses.

Typically, ALE coverage is set as a percentage of your dwelling coverage, usually around 20%. It's important to note that ALE coverage has limits, and some policies also include a time limitation.

Personal Liability Coverage

Personal liability coverage protects you if you're legally responsible for injury or property damage to others. For instance, if a guest falls and gets injured in your home, your liability coverage could help pay for their medical bills or your legal fees if they sue you.

Liability coverage limits usually start at about $100,000, but it may be wise to purchase more coverage if you have significant assets to protect. You can often increase your liability coverage up to $500,000 on a standard policy, or even more if you purchase an umbrella policy.

Medical Payments to Others Coverage

Medical payments to others coverage, often known as "med pay," can pay for minor medical expenses if someone gets injured on your property, regardless of who's at fault. This coverage usually has lower limits and is meant to cover small claims that may not warrant a liability claim. Med pay coverage limits typically range from $1,000 to $5,000.

Understanding Exclusions and Endorsements

While your home insurance policy provides a wide range of coverages, it also has exclusions – specific situations or perils that aren't covered. Common exclusions include damage due to floods, earthquakes, landslides, war, nuclear hazard, and intentional loss.

If you live in an area prone to specific risks like floods or earthquakes, you may need to purchase additional coverage, often called an endorsement or rider, to protect against these perils. An endorsement modifies your policy to provide additional coverage or change the terms of your coverage. It can be a crucial tool for tailoring your insurance policy to fit your unique needs and risks.

Deductibles and Policy Limits

Your home insurance policy will also specify a deductible and policy limits. The deductible is the amount you're required to pay out-of-pocket before your insurance coverage kicks in if you file a claim. Choosing a higher deductible can lower your premium, but it also means you'll pay more out-of-pocket in the event of a claim.

Your policy limits are the maximum amounts your insurance company will pay for a covered loss. Each type of coverage in your policy has its limit. It's essential to set your coverage limits high enough to adequately protect your home, personal property, and assets.

The Importance of Regular Policy Reviews

Finally, it's important to review your home insurance policy regularly, ideally once a year or whenever significant changes occur in your life or home. This helps ensure your coverage keeps pace with changes in your home's value, the cost of construction, and your personal property value. Regular reviews can also help you catch potential coverage gaps, giving you the opportunity to adjust your coverage and limits as necessary.

Conclusion

Your homeowner's insurance policy is your financial defense against unexpected disasters, providing crucial protection for your home, personal property, and assets. Understanding the intricacies of your policy's coverage can help you make informed decisions and ensure you have the protection you need.

By familiarizing yourself with the main components of home insurance coverage – dwelling, other structures, personal property, loss of use, personal liability, and medical payments to others – you're better equipped to review and adjust your policy to fit your needs.

In the following chapters, we'll delve deeper into the ins and outs of each type of coverage, further equipping you to make the best decisions about your home insurance coverage. It's a critical step in safeguarding your most significant investment – your home.

DECIPHERING INSURANCE JARGON: KEY TERMS YOU NEED TO KNOW

Insurance terminology can often seem like a language of its own. To be a well-informed policyholder, it's essential to understand the key terms and phrases associated with your homeowner's insurance. In this chapter, we'll take a deep dive into the critical terms that can help you comprehend your insurance policy better.

1. Policyholder

The policyholder is the person who owns the insurance policy. This person is also responsible for making premium payments and is the one who can make changes to the policy.

2. Premium

The premium is the amount of money you pay to the insurance company in exchange for the coverage provided by your insurance policy. It can be paid annually, semi-annually, or monthly, depending on your agreement with the insurer.

3. Deductible

The deductible is the amount you have to pay out-of-pocket for a loss before your insurance coverage begins to pay. A higher deductible usually results in a lower premium, but it also means you'll pay more out-of-pocket if you file a claim.

4. Claim

A claim is a formal request to an insurance company asking for a payment based on the terms of the insurance policy. When you file a claim, you're requesting the insurance company to repair or replace what's been damaged or lost, according to your policy.

5. Coverage

Coverage refers to the protections and benefits provided by an insurance policy. It spells out what the insurance company agrees to cover in the event of specific losses.

6. Liability

Liability refers to the legal responsibility for one's acts or omissions. In the context of homeowner's insurance, personal liability coverage protects you if you're legally responsible for injury or property damage to others.

7. Peril

A peril is an event that could cause loss or damage, like a fire or theft. Insurance policies can cover certain perils and exclude others.

8. Endorsement

An endorsement, also known as a rider or a floater, is an addition or amendment to an existing insurance policy to either expand or limit the coverage provided by the policy.

9. Exclusion

Exclusions are specific conditions or circumstances for which the policy will not provide coverage. Common exclusions in a homeowner's insurance policy include damage caused by floods, earthquakes, or routine wear and tear.

10. Actual Cash Value (ACV)

Actual Cash Value is the cost to replace an item with a similar one at current market prices, minus depreciation. In other words, it's the value of the item at the time of the loss, not the price you paid for it or the cost to replace it with a new one.

11. Replacement Cost Vaiue (RCV)

Replacement Cost Value is the cost to replace the lost or damaged property with new property of similar kind and quality, without any deduction for depreciation.

12. Depreciation

Depreciation is the decrease in the value of an item over time, primarily due to wear and tear. It's taken into account when determining the actual cash value of a property.

13. Underwriting

Underwriting is the process through which an insurer determines the risk of providing insurance to a home or individual. The underwriter decides whether to provide insurance, how much coverage to offer, and at what price.

14. Binder

A binder is a temporary insurance contract that provides proof of coverage until a formal policy is issued.

15. Subrogation

Subrogation is the process by which an insurance company seeks repayment from the party at fault for the damages it paid to the insured.

Conclusion

Understanding insurance jargon is a key step towards being a well-informed policyholder and making the most of your homeowner's insurance. By familiarizing yourself with these terms, you're better equipped to understand your policy, ask the right questions, and make informed decisions about your insurance coverage.

Additionally, understanding these terms can help you effectively navigate the claims process. If you ever need to file a claim, being fluent in insurance terminology can enable you to communicate effectively with your insurance provider and understand the processes involved.

Keep in mind that your insurance agent or representative is also a valuable resource. If you encounter a term or concept in your policy that you don't understand, don't hesitate to ask for clarification. As a consumer, you have the right to understand the contract you're entering into fully. It's part of your insurance company's responsibility to ensure that you do.

As we move forward into subsequent chapters, we'll delve deeper into each component of your home insurance policy and explore topics like how to file a claim, what to do after a loss, and how to maintain your home to prevent common insurance claims. Equipped with your newfound understanding of insurance jargon, you'll be prepared to grasp these topics and apply them to your unique insurance needs and situation.

By fully understanding these key terms, you can ensure you're utilizing your homeowner's insurance policy to its fullest extent. It's an essential aspect of protecting your most significant investment – your home.

LIABILITY COVERAGE: PROTECTING YOU FROM LEGAL HASSLES

Liability coverage is an often overlooked, yet critical, part of your homeowner's insurance policy. It protects you from the financial fallout of accidents or injuries that occur on your property for which you're legally responsible. In this chapter, we'll explore the importance of liability coverage, its components, and how it functions in real-world scenarios.

Understanding Liability Coverage

At its core, personal liability coverage in your homeowner's insurance policy is designed to cover legal and medical costs if someone gets injured on your property and you're found at fault. This might include situations like a visitor tripping over a loose carpet and getting injured or your dog biting a neighbor.

Liability coverage is typically divided into two parts: Personal Liability Coverage and Medical Payments to Others Coverage.

Personal Liability Coverage

Personal Liability Coverage provides protection if you're found legally responsible for an accident that causes injury or property damage to someone else. It can cover the costs of medical bills, repair or replacement costs, and your legal expenses if the injured party decides to sue.

Suppose a neighbor's child falls off a trampoline in your backyard and breaks a leg. Personal liability coverage can help cover the child's medical costs. And if the parents decide to sue you for the accident, this coverage could also help cover your legal expenses, up to the limits of your policy.

Medical Payments to Others Coverage

Medical Payments to Others Coverage, often known as "med pay," can pay for minor medical expenses if someone outside your household gets injured on your property, regardless of who's at fault. This coverage is usually available in smaller amounts, such as $1,000 to $5,000, and is designed to cover small claims that may not warrant a liability claim.

For example, if a friend gets a minor cut while helping you chop vegetables in your kitchen, med pay could cover the costs of their emergency room visit.

Importance of Adequate Liability Coverage

Having adequate liability coverage is crucial because accidents and lawsuits can be incredibly costly. Without adequate coverage, you might have to pay these costs out of pocket, potentially leading to financial hardship.

Most standard homeowner's insurance policies offer a minimum of $100,000 in liability coverage, but many experts recommend carrying at least $300,000 to $500,000 in coverage, depending on your personal circumstances. If you have significant assets, you might even consider purchasing an umbrella policy, which provides additional liability coverage above the limits of your standard homeowner's insurance policy.

Umbrella Policy: Extra Layer of Protection

An umbrella policy provides liability coverage above and beyond the limits of your homeowner's insurance. If you're sued for a significant amount that exceeds the liability coverage of your home insurance, your umbrella policy can cover the remaining balance, up to the limits of the policy.

Umbrella policies usually start at $1 million in coverage and can go up from there. They're generally affordable, especially considering the amount of coverage they provide, and can offer peace of mind if you have significant assets to protect.

Conclusion

Liability coverage is a critical part of your homeowner's insurance policy that can protect you from the financial fallout of accidents or injuries on your property. By understanding how this coverage works and ensuring you have adequate protection, you can safeguard your financial well-being and maintain your peace of mind.

In the upcoming chapters, we will delve into other critical aspects of homeowner's insurance, such as filing a claim, disaster preparedness, and policy renewal. With a solid understanding of liability coverage under your belt, you'll be better equipped to navigate these topics and to ensure your homeowner's insurance policy is working effectively to protect you, your home, and your financial future.

NATURAL DISASTERS AND HOME INSURANCE: ARE YOU FULLY COVERED?

Natural disasters such as hurricanes, wildfires, and earthquakes can cause significant damage to your home. Ensuring that your homeowner's insurance provides adequate coverage for these events is crucial. This chapter will explore how home insurance typically handles natural disasters, common exclusions, and additional coverage options you may need to consider.

Home Insurance and Natural Disasters: The Basics

Standard homeowner's insurance policies typically cover damage caused by certain natural disasters, often referred to as perils. These can include fire, windstorms, hail, lightning, and volcanic eruptions. However, it's important to note that while these perils are generally covered, every policy has limits - the maximum amount your insurance company will pay towards a covered loss.

For instance, if a lightning strike causes a fire in your home, your policy would generally pay to repair or rebuild your home, up to the policy's limits for dwelling coverage. It would also typically cover damage to your personal belongings, under the personal property coverage.

However, not all natural disasters are covered by a standard homeowner's insurance policy.

Common Exclusions: Floods and Earthquakes

Two of the most common natural disaster exclusions in standard home insurance policies are floods and earthquakes. This means that if your home is damaged or destroyed by a flood or earthquake, your standard homeowner's insurance wouldn't cover the damage.

Flood Insurance

Flood insurance is typically purchased as a separate policy. In the U.S., flood insurance is often obtained through the National Flood Insurance Program (NFIP), which is managed by the Federal Emergency Management Agency (FEMA). Private flood insurance is also available from some insurance companies.

Flood insurance covers damage to your home and personal property caused by flooding, up to the policy's limits. There are separate coverage limits for building property and personal property, and certain items like valuable artwork may require additional coverage.

Earthquake Insurance

Like flood insurance, earthquake insurance is typically purchased as a separate policy or an endorsement to your standard home insurance policy. It covers damage to your home and personal belongings caused by an earthquake, up to the policy's limits. Some policies may also cover additional living expenses if you have to live elsewhere while your home is being repaired or rebuilt.

Other Exclusions and Considerations

While floods and earthquakes are common exclusions, other natural disasters may also be excluded, depending on where you live. For instance, some policies may not cover windstorm or hail damage if you live in a hurricane-prone area. Or, if you live in a wildfire-prone area, your insurer may limit coverage for fire damage.

To ensure you're adequately covered, it's crucial to review your policy carefully, understand its exclusions, and consider additional coverage based on your home's location and your area's risk of natural disasters.

Conclusion

While your homeowner's insurance policy provides coverage for many types of natural disasters, it doesn't cover everything. Knowing what your policy covers, what it excludes, and what additional coverage options are available to you can help ensure you're adequately protected.

In the upcoming chapters, we'll delve into other crucial aspects of homeowner's insurance, such as how to file a claim, what to do after a disaster, and how to prepare for renewing your policy. By understanding how your home insurance policy handles natural disasters, you're better equipped to navigate these topics and ensure your most valuable investment - your home - is fully protected.

THE ROLE OF HOME IMPROVEMENTS AND RENOVATIONS IN YOUR COVERAGE

Home improvements and renovations not only add value to your home but also often necessitate a review and potential update of your home insurance policy. Whether you're remodeling your kitchen, adding a new room, or installing a pool, these changes can impact the adequacy of your coverage. In this chapter, we'll delve into the relationship between home improvements and your homeowner's insurance.

Understanding the Impact of Home Improvements on Home Insurance

The essence of homeowner's insurance is to provide financial protection against potential damage to your home. When you make substantial improvements or renovations, you're essentially changing the value of your home, which could render your existing coverage inadequate.

For instance, if you remodel your kitchen with high-end appliances and finishes, the cost to rebuild your home in case of a disaster may increase. If your policy isn't updated to reflect these changes, you could be left with a coverage gap that could lead to significant out-of-pocket expenses in the event of a claim.

Informing Your Insurance Company about Home Improvements

It's crucial to inform your insurance company about any planned or completed renovations or improvements to ensure you maintain adequate coverage. They can reassess your home's value and adjust your coverage accordingly. This might result in an increase in your premium, but it would also provide you with better protection for your updated home.

Moreover, some improvements might even lead to discounts on your insurance premium. For example, a new roof, updated electrical, plumbing, or HVAC systems might qualify for discounts since they reduce the likelihood of damage and potential claims.

Consideration of Liability Risks

Certain home improvements can increase your liability risk, meaning they might increase the chances of someone getting injured on your property. The addition of a swimming pool, trampoline, or even certain breeds of dogs can significantly increase your liability risk.

In these cases, you'll want to review your liability coverage to ensure it's sufficient to protect you in case of an accident. You may also want to consider an umbrella policy for additional liability coverage.

Replacement Cost vs. Actual Cash Value

When reviewing your policy following a home improvement, consider whether your policy offers replacement cost or actual cash value coverage. Replacement cost coverage pays to replace or repair your home with materials of similar kind and quality, without considering depreciation. On the other hand, actual cash value coverage factors in depreciation and only pays for the value of your home at the time of the loss.

Replacement cost coverage can provide better protection, especially after a significant home improvement. If your current policy offers actual cash value coverage, you might want to consider upgrading to replacement cost coverage.

Conclusion

Home improvements and renovations can significantly impact your homeowner's insurance. By informing your insurer about these changes, reassessing the value of your home, and adjusting your coverage, you can ensure that your policy continues to provide the protection you need.

In the following chapters, we'll explore other aspects of homeowner's insurance, such as how to file a claim and navigating the claims process, preparing for policy renewal, and maintaining your home to prevent insurance claims. By understanding the role of home improvements in your coverage, you can make informed decisions about your policy and continue to protect your most significant investment – your home.

THE IMPACT OF LOCATION AND NEIGHBORHOOD ON YOUR INSURANCE PREMIUM

The location of your home significantly impacts your homeowner's insurance premium. Factors like proximity to a fire station, crime rates, and risk of natural disasters in your neighborhood all play a role in determining your rates. Understanding these factors can help you make informed decisions when purchasing a home or reviewing your insurance needs.

Proximity to a Fire Station

Insurance companies assess the risk of fire damage to your home based on how quickly a fire can be responded to. A home closer to a fire station typically has a lower risk, which can translate to lower insurance premiums. Similarly, proximity to a fire hydrant also affects your rate, as it determines how readily a fire can be extinguished.

Crime Rates in Your Neighborhood

The higher the crime rate in your area, the higher the risk of vandalism or theft, leading to higher premiums. Insurance companies often use crime statistics when determining premiums. Therefore, living in a neighborhood with low crime rates could potentially decrease your insurance costs.

Natural Disasters Risk

The risk of natural disasters varies widely based on location. If your home is in an area prone to floods, earthquakes, hurricanes, or wildfires, your insurance premium is likely to be higher. For example, homes in California are at a higher risk of earthquake and wildfire damage, while homes in Florida are at a higher risk of hurricane damage. In many cases, you may also need to purchase additional coverage for these specific risks, as they may not be covered by a standard home insurance policy.

Building Material and Construction Quality

The materials used in building your home and the quality of construction can affect how it withstands damage and therefore impact your insurance premium. For example, brick homes are generally more resistant to fire damage than wood-frame homes, which could lead to lower insurance premiums in areas where fire risk is high.

On the other hand, in earthquake-prone areas, wood-frame homes that can flex during an earthquake might be less risky, and hence cheaper to insure, than brick homes, which could crack or crumble.

Nearby Amenities

Certain nearby amenities can also impact your home insurance premium. For example, living near a high-risk industry such as a power plant could raise your rates due to the potential risk of environmental damage.

Similarly, if your neighborhood has a high number of short-term rentals or unoccupied homes, insurers may view this as an increased risk for theft or vandalism, potentially raising your rates.

Conclusion

The location of your home and the characteristics of your neighborhood significantly impact your home insurance premium. Understanding these factors can help you make informed decisions when buying a home, choosing an insurance policy, or improving your home's safety features to potentially lower your premiums.

In the next chapter, we will dive into the details of the insurance claims process, including how to file a claim, what to expect during the process, and tips for making it as smooth as possible. With the foundation of understanding we've built about how various factors influence your insurance premium, you'll be well-prepared to navigate these next topics with confidence.

UNDERSTANDING DEDUCTIBLES AND PREMIUMS: THE FINE BALANCE

Deductibles and premiums are two key elements of your homeowner's insurance policy. Both directly impact the cost of your insurance and the level of your coverage. Understanding the relationship between the two helps you make informed decisions about your policy. In this chapter, we'll explore the balance between deductibles and premiums and how adjustments can affect your coverage.

The Basics: Deductibles and Premiums

Firstly, let's define these two terms. A deductible is the amount you're responsible for paying out of pocket before your insurance coverage kicks in if a loss occurs. The premium, on the other hand, is the amount you pay to the insurance company, usually on a monthly or annual basis, to maintain your coverage.

The Relationship between Deductibles and Premiums

The relationship between deductibles and premiums is inversely proportional. A higher deductible generally leads to a lower premium and vice versa. The reasoning is simple: if you choose a high deductible, you're taking on more financial responsibility in the event of a claim. Consequently, the insurance company bears less risk, which results in a lower premium.

Conversely, if you opt for a lower deductible, your insurer assumes more of the financial risk, resulting in a higher premium. Essentially, when you choose a lower deductible, you're transferring more risk to the insurance company, and that comes at a cost.

Choosing the Right Balance

Finding the right balance between your deductible and your premium largely depends on your financial situation and risk tolerance. If you have enough savings to cover a higher deductible and prefer lower regular payments, choosing a higher deductible might be a suitable choice for you. On the other hand, if you would find it challenging to cover a high deductible after a loss, it might be better to opt for a lower deductible and a slightly higher premium.

Remember, the purpose of insurance is to protect you from large, unexpected financial losses. If paying a high deductible would put you in a financial bind, it would be wise to consider a lower deductible.

Deductibles for Different Types of Claims

It's important to note that some policies may have different deductibles for different types of claims. For instance, if you live in a hurricane-prone area, your policy might have a separate, usually higher, deductible for hurricane-related claims.

Make sure you understand any separate deductibles in your policy, as they could significantly impact your out-of-pocket costs in the event of a claim.

Annual Review and Adjustments

Your financial situation and risk tolerance can change over time, so it's essential to review your deductible and premium annually. If your financial circumstances have improved, you may choose to increase your deductible and reduce your premium. Alternatively, if you're less able to absorb financial shocks, you may opt to reduce your deductible, even if it means a slight increase in your premium.

Conclusion

Balancing deductibles and premiums is a crucial part of managing your homeowner's insurance policy. Understanding the relationship between the two can help you make informed decisions that best fit your financial situation and risk tolerance.

In the upcoming chapters, we'll delve into further important aspects of homeowner's insurance, including how to file and navigate a claim, disaster preparedness, and preparing for your policy renewal. With the understanding of the balance between deductibles and premiums, you'll be better equipped to navigate these topics and ensure your insurance coverage effectively protects your most significant investment—your home.

THE CLAIMS PROCESS: FROM DAMAGE TO REIMBURSEMENT

When the unexpected happens, your homeowner's insurance policy is there to provide financial protection. Filing a claim can be a stressful process, especially when you're dealing with damage to your home. This chapter aims to shed light on the steps involved in the claims process, from damage assessment to reimbursement, and provide helpful tips to ensure the process runs smoothly.

Step 1: Assess the Damage

The first step after an incident is to assess the damage. Determine if the situation requires immediate intervention and if so, take necessary action to prevent further damage. This might involve calling in a professional to deal with water damage or boarding up windows after a storm. Be sure to take photos or videos of the damage for your records.

Step 2: Review Your Policy

Before filing a claim, review your insurance policy to understand your coverage limits, deductible, and whether the type of damage you've suffered is covered.

Understanding the terms of your policy will help you set realistic expectations for the claim process.

Step 3: Contact Your Insurance Company

Next, contact your insurance company as soon as possible to report the loss. The insurance company will assign an adjuster to your claim, who will be your primary point of contact. They will guide you through the process, inspect the damage, and determine the amount of compensation you're entitled to under your policy.

Step 4: Document and Report the Damage

Provide your adjuster with the photos or videos of the damage, along with any other documentation they might need. This might include receipts for damaged items or estimates for repair work. Your adjuster will use this information, along with their inspection, to estimate the cost of the damage.

Step 5: Adjustment

The adjuster will carry out a thorough inspection of the reported damage to confirm what repairs are necessary and how much they will cost. They will compare this with your policy details to determine how much the insurance company will pay.

Step 6: Settlement

Once the adjuster completes their assessment, they will provide a settlement based on the coverage in your policy. If you agree with their assessment, you can accept the settlement. However, if you disagree, you can negotiate or hire a public adjuster to advocate on your behalf.

Step 7: Reimbursement

After a settlement is reached, the insurance company will reimburse you for the covered damage, minus your deductible. Depending on your policy, this might be in the form of an actual cash value or a replacement cost.

Tips for a Smooth Claims Process

Document everything: Keep a record of every interaction with your insurance company, including dates, names, and the nature of the discussion.

Be proactive: Don't hesitate to ask questions and make sure you fully understand each step of the process.

Consider a public adjuster: If you feel overwhelmed by the process or are unsatisfied with the insurance company's adjuster, consider hiring a public adjuster.

Conclusion

The claims process can be a complex journey, but understanding the steps involved can make it less daunting. By being prepared and proactive, you can navigate the process and ensure you receive the compensation you're entitled to.

In the coming chapters, we'll cover further essential aspects of homeowner's insurance, including disaster preparedness, maintenance to prevent claims, and preparing for policy renewal. With a good understanding of the claims process, you'll be well-equipped to navigate these areas and ensure your insurance policy serves its purpose - protecting your most significant investment, your home.

TIPS FOR MAKING A SUCCESSFUL INSURANCE CLAIM

Filing an insurance claim may seem daunting, particularly when you're dealing with the stress of damage to your home. But understanding how to effectively navigate the process can ease your concerns and enhance your chances of making a successful claim. This chapter will provide you with practical tips to guide you from the moment you notice damage through to final settlement.

Tip 1: Understand Your Policy

Before a disaster strikes, make sure you have a good understanding of what your insurance policy covers. Read it thoroughly and discuss any unclear areas with your insurance agent. Be aware of any exclusions or limitations, understand the amount of your deductible, and know the difference between replacement cost and actual cash value in your policy.

Tip 2: Prompt Reporting

When you notice damage, it's essential to report it to your insurer as soon as possible. Most insurance policies require prompt reporting of any losses. Not only does this help to prevent further damage, but it also means that the claim process can begin immediately.

Tip 3: Document Everything

Documentation is key in the claims process. Start by taking photos or videos of the damage before you clean up or make temporary repairs. Keep a record of all communication with your insurer, including dates, the names of the people you speak with, and what was discussed. Maintain a list of damaged or lost items, along with their approximate value. If possible, provide receipts, photos, or other proof of ownership.

Tip 4: Make Necessary Temporary Repairs

To prevent further damage, you may need to make temporary repairs, like covering a broken window or leaking roof. Be sure to discuss these repairs with your insurance company first, keep all receipts, and take "before and after" photos to document the damage and repairs.

Tip 5: Work Closely With Your Adjuster

Your insurance adjuster is your main point of contact during the claims process. They will inspect the damage, review your documentation, and determine the amount of your claim. Be cooperative and provide any information they need. If you're unsure about something, don't hesitate to ask questions.

Tip 6: Be Honest and Complete

It's crucial to provide accurate and complete information about the damage and your losses. Honesty is not only ethical but also ensures a smoother process. Remember, false or exaggerated claims can lead to denial of the claim or even policy cancellation.

Tip 7: Don't Rush the Settlement

While you may want to have the process over and done with quickly, it's crucial not to rush the settlement. Make sure you agree with the adjuster's assessment of the damage and the estimated repair costs. If you disagree, don't hesitate to negotiate or seek a second opinion.

Tip 8: Seek Professional Help If Needed

If your claim is complicated or if you're not comfortable handling it yourself, consider seeking help. This could be a public adjuster or an attorney who specializes in insurance claims.

Conclusion

While the insurance claims process can be challenging, following these tips can increase your chances of making a successful claim. Remember that understanding your policy, documenting thoroughly, and maintaining open communication with your insurer are key factors in navigating this process.

In the subsequent chapters, we'll delve into more aspects of home insurance, such as preparing for natural disasters, maintaining your home to prevent claims, and preparing for your policy renewal. Armed with these tips for making a successful insurance claim, you'll be in a stronger position to ensure your policy works effectively for you, safeguarding your most significant asset – your home.

HOME INSURANCE FOR CONDOS AND TOWNHOUSES: WHAT'S DIFFERENT?

Owning a condo or townhouse involves different responsibilities compared to owning a traditional, detached home, and these differences extend to insurance needs. Condo and townhouse owners often find themselves asking, "What's different about our home insurance?" This chapter will elucidate the distinctions and detail how condo and townhouse insurance work, guiding you towards an insurance policy that fits your needs.

Part 1: Understanding Condo Insurance

What is Condo Insurance?

Condo insurance, also known as HO-6 insurance, provides coverage for the inside of your condominium. It offers protection for your personal property and the interior of your unit, plus liability coverage in case someone is injured on your property.

What Does Condo Insurance Cover?

Typically, condo insurance covers the following:

- Personal Property: This covers belongings inside your condo, like furniture, electronics, and clothing.
- Interior of Your Unit: This covers fixtures and structural parts of the inside of your condo, such as flooring, countertops, and built-in appliances.
- Personal Liability: This protects you if someone is injured on your property or if you accidentally damage another unit.
- Loss of Use: This covers additional living expenses if you're forced to temporarily move out due to a covered loss.

What About the Rest of the Building?

The physical structure of the condo building, along with common areas like the lobby, elevator, and gym, are generally covered by the condo association's master policy. It's crucial to understand what the master policy covers so you can adequately insure your unit. Master policies can be "all-in" (covering fixtures in your unit like sinks and toilets) or "walls-in" (covering only the bare walls, floors, and ceiling).

Part 2: Understanding Townhouse Insurance

What is Townhouse Insurance?

Townhouse insurance, typically a standard homeowners insurance policy (HO-3), provides comprehensive coverage for your townhouse structure, personal property, and liability. This is because, unlike condo owners, townhouse owners usually own the structure of their home.

What Does Townhouse Insurance Cover?

Townhouse insurance commonly covers the following:

Physical Structure: This covers damage to the structure of your townhouse from covered perils like fire, theft, or storm damage.

Personal Property: This includes coverage for personal belongings inside your townhouse.

Liability Protection: This protects you against legal issues arising from injuries or damage caused to others on your property.

Additional Living Expenses: If a covered peril forces you out of your home, this helps cover your temporary living costs.

Similar to a condo association's master policy, the HOA might have a policy that covers damage to the exterior of the townhouse buildings and common areas. As a townhouse owner, it's essential to understand what your HOA policy covers so you can adjust your personal insurance coverage accordingly.

Part 3: Condos vs. Townhouses: The Key Difference

The main difference in insurance for condos and townhouses lies in the ownership of the structure. Since condo owners typically only own the interior of their units, their insurance is focused on covering the inside and their personal belongings. In contrast, townhouse owners usually own the structure of their homes, so they require a policy that covers the full structure, much like a detached home.

Conclusion

Understanding the unique needs of condo and townhouse insurance is crucial to ensuring that you are adequately covered. It's important to understand not just your insurance policy, but also the coverage provided by your condo association's master policy or your homeowners association (HOA) policy. This dual-layer of insurance may seem complex, but it's designed to provide a comprehensive safeguard for your property.

While the distinction between condo insurance and townhouse insurance is clear, there is another factor to consider – the type of coverage provided by the master or HOA policy. For instance, if the master policy is a "bare walls" policy, you'll need to ensure that your personal condo insurance covers things like installed fixtures and interior renovations. If the master or HOA policy is "all-inclusive," your personal policy might only need to cover your personal belongings and provide liability coverage.

Communication is key in understanding these intricacies. Regular discussions with your HOA or condo association, and your insurance agent, can help clear any confusion and ensure your coverage meets your needs.

Additionally, it's worth remembering that just as with traditional homeowners insurance, the cost of condo and townhouse insurance can vary depending on factors such as location, the value of your personal belongings, the materials used in construction, and the level of security in your building or complex.

Lastly, whether you own a condo or a townhouse, it's crucial to periodically review and update your insurance coverage. Personal situations can change – maybe you've acquired valuable new belongings, or perhaps you've undertaken major renovations. Regularly reviewing your policy ensures it keeps pace with your life changes and continues to provide the protection you need.

Insurance for condos and townhouses doesn't have to be confusing. Once you understand the differences and your unique needs, you can find a policy that provides peace of mind, knowing that your home is well protected.

In the coming chapters, we'll delve further into essential topics of home insurance, such as insurance for rental properties, how to prepare for natural disasters, and the process of policy renewal. By understanding the specific considerations for condos and townhouses, you'll be better equipped to navigate these areas and ensure your insurance coverage is comprehensive, relevant, and well-suited to your property type.

THE INTRICACIES OF INSURANCE FOR HISTORIC AND HIGH-VALUE HOMES

Historic and high-value homes are unique pieces of property that often come with intricate detailing, valuable structures, and rich histories. Such properties need a specialized type of insurance coverage that acknowledges their exceptional characteristics. This chapter aims to elucidate the complexities of insuring these unique homes, providing insights into considerations and best practices.

Part 1: Insuring Historic Homes

What Makes Historic Homes Unique?

Historic homes are not just older houses; they are structures of significant cultural, historical, or architectural value. They might be officially listed on a national or local historic register or located in a designated historic district. Due to their historic status, these homes often require specific care, maintenance, and restoration processes that can be quite expensive.

Understanding Historic Home Insurance

Standard homeowners insurance may not offer adequate coverage for historic homes. Specialized historic home insurance recognizes the unique needs of these properties. It typically covers the cost to repair or rebuild the home to its original, historical condition after a covered loss.

Considerations When Insuring Historic Homes

- Restoration Costs: Historic homes usually require specialized materials and skilled craftspeople for restoration. This means repair costs could be significantly higher than a standard home.
- Building Codes and Regulations: Historic homes often have to comply with preservation standards and local building regulations, which can increase the cost of repairs.
- Ordinance or Law Coverage: This provides coverage for the increased costs due to enforcing any ordinance or law regulating the construction, repair, or demolition of buildings.
- Historic Value: Coverage should account for the home's historic value, including unique architectural details.

Part 2: Insuring High-Value Homes

What are High-Value Homes?

High-value homes, as the name implies, are properties with a high market value—usually significantly higher than the average home price in their location. They often include luxury features like custom architecture, top-of-the-line kitchens, art collections, wine cellars, and more.

Understanding High-Value Home Insurance

High-value home insurance is designed to offer coverage limits and features that meet the unique needs of high-value properties. It often includes higher limits for dwelling and personal property coverage, as well as expanded coverage for things like collections, identity theft, and even kidnap and ransom in some cases.

Considerations When Insuring High-Value Homes

- Appraisal: Regular appraisals are critical to ensure the insurance coverage matches the home's current value.
- Custom Coverage: High-value homes often require custom coverage to protect luxury features.

- High-Limits Coverage: High-value home insurance usually offers higher limits, especially for personal liability coverage.

Conclusion

Insuring historic and high-value homes can be complex, but with the right approach, you can ensure your unique property is adequately protected. Partnering with an experienced insurance agent who specializes in these types of homes can be a significant advantage.

Keep in mind that, as a homeowner, you have the responsibility to understand your coverage needs and to work with your agent to meet those needs. This includes keeping your agent informed about any changes to your home, such as renovations, the acquisition of valuable items, or any factors that may increase the value of your home.

Remember, while the cost of insurance for historic and high-value homes can be high, the cost of not having adequate coverage can be significantly higher.

In the upcoming chapters, we'll delve into more crucial aspects of home insurance, including the nuances of insuring rental properties, preparing for policy renewal, and mitigating common risks. Understanding the intricacies of insuring historic and high-value homes can give you a deeper insight into the various aspects of home insurance and can guide you in navigating these scenarios with confidence.

Whether you own a grand historic home with intricate Victorian detailing or a modern high-value home filled with custom finishes and art collections, you'll understand that these properties require more than just standard coverage. They need a specialized approach, a comprehensive understanding of their value, and a policy that ensures their distinctive features are adequately protected.

Insuring these homes is not just about protecting a dwelling; it's about safeguarding a piece of history or an embodiment of luxury. It's about preserving architectural heritage in the case of historic homes, and maintaining a lifestyle and protecting valuable possessions in the case of high-value homes. Your insurance coverage should reflect these aspects and provide you with peace of mind, knowing that your unique home has the protection it deserves.

This comprehensive understanding of insurance nuances will be beneficial as we continue exploring different facets of home insurance. From learning about liability coverage to understanding how natural disasters can impact your home and insurance, the information provided will help you navigate the world of home insurance effectively.

Historic and high-value homes, with their unique charm and distinct needs, have a lot to teach us about the vast and intricate realm of home insurance. By understanding these, you are better equipped to make informed decisions, ensuring that your policy offers the protection that aligns perfectly with your unique home and lifestyle.

NAVIGATING HOME INSURANCE WITH PETS AND UNUSUAL RISKS

Pets, though a source of joy and companionship, can introduce a degree of uncertainty and risk when it comes to home insurance. Similarly, unusual risks, such as owning a trampoline or a swimming pool, can complicate your home insurance situation. This chapter will guide you through navigating home insurance with these potential risks in mind.

Part 1: Insuring a Home with Pets

The Role of Pets in Home Insurance

Pets can potentially cause damage to your property or injure someone, which could lead to an insurance claim. As such, the breed of your pet, its history, and its behavior can influence your home insurance.

Considerations When Insuring a Home with Pets

- Breed Considerations: Some insurance companies have lists of breeds they consider 'high-risk' due to statistical data on breed-specific behavior. These

breeds may lead to higher premiums or even policy denial.
- Liability Coverage: Your home insurance should include adequate liability coverage to protect you if your pet injures someone or damages their property.
- Disclosing Pet Ownership: Always disclose pet ownership to your insurer. Non-disclosure can lead to denied claims or even policy cancellation.

Part 2: Addressing Unusual Risks

Identifying Unusual Risks

Unusual risks refer to elements that increase the likelihood of injury or property damage. Examples include owning a swimming pool, a trampoline, or even certain types of landscaping. It's important to identify these risks and discuss them with your insurance provider.

Considerations for Insuring Homes with Unusual Risks

- Liability Coverage: Unusual risks can increase your liability exposure. Make sure your policy provides sufficient coverage for any incidents related to these risks.

- Risk Mitigation: Implement safety measures to minimize these risks, such as installing a fence around a swimming pool or providing adequate supervision when a trampoline is in use.
- Disclosing Unusual Risks: Always inform your insurance company about these risks. Failure to do so may result in denied claims.

Conclusion

Navigating home insurance with pets and unusual risks doesn't have to be a daunting process. Open communication with your insurance provider is key. Disclosing all relevant information, from your pet's breed to the existence of a backyard pool, can prevent future complications and ensure you have the coverage you need.

Remember, insurance is there to protect you and your assets. While pets and certain home features may present additional challenges, they can still be accommodated within a comprehensive home insurance plan. It's about understanding these risks, mitigating them wherever possible, and having an insurance policy that takes them into account.

In the following chapters, we'll explore more about the world of home insurance, from the unique considerations for rental properties to preparing for policy renewal and understanding your rights as a policyholder. By comprehending how pets and unusual risks can impact your home insurance, you'll be better prepared to navigate these areas and ensure your coverage is fit for purpose.

Whether you're a pet owner, a pool owner, or both, understanding the relationship between these elements and your home insurance is crucial. By applying the knowledge from this chapter, you'll be able to strike a balance between enjoying the companionship of your pets, making the most of your home's features, and maintaining an insurance policy that provides you with the security and peace of mind you need.

BUNDLING HOME INSURANCE WITH OTHER POLICIES: PROS AND CONS

Bundling your home insurance with other insurance policies, such as auto insurance or umbrella insurance, can offer convenience and potentially save you money. However, it's essential to understand the pros and cons of bundling to make an informed decision. This chapter explores the advantages and disadvantages of bundling your home insurance with other policies.

Part 1: The Pros of Bundling

Convenience and Simplification

Bundling your home insurance with other policies can provide convenience and simplify your insurance management. By having multiple policies with a single insurance company, you'll have one point of contact for your insurance needs, making it easier to manage your policies, pay premiums, and handle claims.

Cost Savings

One of the primary advantages of bundling insurance policies is the potential for cost savings. Insurance companies often offer discounts when you bundle multiple policies with them. These discounts can lead to significant savings on your premiums, making bundling an attractive option for many homeowners.

Increased Coverage

In addition to potential cost savings, bundling policies can also provide increased coverage. When you bundle, you may have access to broader coverage options or higher coverage limits that might not be available when purchasing individual policies. This enhanced coverage can provide better protection for your home and assets.

Part 2: The Cons of Bundling

Limited Options for Comparison

One of the drawbacks of bundling is that it limits your ability to compare policies from different insurance providers. Bundling may lead you to focus solely on the bundled price and discounts, potentially preventing you from exploring other insurance options that may offer better coverage or pricing for specific policies.

Loss of Flexibility

Bundling can limit your flexibility to make changes to your insurance coverage. If you want to switch insurance providers for a specific policy or adjust coverage on one policy while keeping others intact, bundling may restrict your ability to do so. This lack of flexibility could become a disadvantage if your insurance needs change over time.

Dependency on a Single Insurer

By bundling policies, you become dependent on a single insurance company for all your coverage needs. While this can simplify management, it also means that if you encounter issues with the insurer, such as poor customer service or uncompetitive pricing, it affects all your policies, including your home insurance.

Part 3: Factors to Consider when Bundling

Insurance Provider Reputation: Research the reputation and financial stability of the insurance company before bundling your policies. Ensure they have a good track record in claims handling and customer service.

- Coverage Suitability: Evaluate whether the coverage provided by the bundled policies adequately meets your specific needs. Don't compromise on coverage just for the sake of bundling.

- Discounts and Pricing: Compare the bundled price and discounts offered by the insurance company with the costs of individual policies from other providers. Ensure the bundled pricing is competitive and provides genuine savings.

- Flexibility and Portability: Consider how bundling might limit your ability to make changes or switch insurance providers in the future. Assess whether the potential loss of flexibility outweighs the convenience of bundling.

Conclusion

Bundling home insurance with other policies can offer convenience, cost savings, and increased coverage. However, it's important to weigh the pros and cons carefully before making a decision. Consider factors such as the reputation of the insurance provider, suitability of coverage, pricing, and the potential loss of flexibility.

In the upcoming chapters, we'll explore further aspects of home insurance, such as understanding the claims process, disaster preparedness, and maintaining your home to prevent claims. Armed with a comprehensive understanding of bundling home insurance with other policies, you'll be better equipped to make informed decisions about your insurance coverage.

Remember to thoroughly assess your insurance needs and compare options from different providers before deciding to bundle your policies. While the convenience and potential cost savings can be appealing, it's crucial to ensure that the bundled coverage meets your specific requirements and provides adequate protection for your home and assets.

Additionally, regularly reassess your insurance needs and review your bundled policies to ensure they align with any changes in your circumstances or risk profile. Periodically reviewing your coverage and comparing it with alternatives in the market can help you determine if bundling continues to be the most suitable option for you.

Lastly, don't hesitate to seek guidance from an insurance professional or independent agent who can provide personalized advice based on your unique situation. They can help you navigate the complexities of bundling, understand the terms and conditions of your policies, and ensure that your insurance coverage is comprehensive and tailored to your needs.

By carefully weighing the pros and cons, considering your specific circumstances, and staying informed about available options, you can make an informed decision about bundling your home insurance with other policies. With the right approach, bundling can provide convenience, cost savings, and enhanced coverage, ensuring that your home and assets are well protected.

In the upcoming chapters, we'll delve into more essential topics of home insurance, such as disaster preparedness, maintaining your home to prevent claims, and preparing for your policy renewal. By expanding your knowledge and understanding of these areas, you'll be well-equipped to navigate the world of home insurance effectively and make informed decisions to protect your most significant investment – your home.

PREVENTATIVE MEASURES: REDUCING RISK AND LOWERING PREMIUMS

Home insurance provides vital financial protection for your property, but taking proactive steps to prevent damage and minimize risks can also contribute to a safer and more affordable insurance experience. This chapter focuses on preventative measures you can take to reduce risk and potentially lower your insurance premiums.

Part 1: Home Safety and Security

Implementing safety measures within your home can significantly reduce the risk of accidents, damage, and theft. Here are some key areas to consider:

- Home Security Systems: Installing a monitored security system can deter burglars and help reduce the risk of theft. Many insurance companies offer discounts for homes equipped with security systems.

- Smoke and Carbon Monoxide Detectors: Properly functioning smoke detectors and carbon monoxide detectors are essential for early detection of fires and harmful gas leaks. Regularly test these devices and replace batteries as needed.

- Fire Prevention: Take preventive measures against fires, such as installing fire extinguishers, maintaining a fire-safe landscape, and ensuring proper storage of flammable materials.

- Home Maintenance: Regularly inspect your home for potential hazards or maintenance issues, such as faulty wiring, plumbing leaks, or deteriorating structures. Promptly address these issues to prevent accidents and damage.

Part 2: Disaster Preparedness

Being prepared for natural disasters can mitigate risks and potentially reduce the impact on your property. Consider the following:

- Hurricane Preparedness: If you live in a hurricane-prone area, reinforce your home with storm shutters, secure outdoor furniture, and ensure your insurance coverage includes adequate protection against wind and flood damage.

- Earthquake Readiness: If you reside in an earthquake-prone region, take steps to secure heavy objects, install earthquake straps for water heaters, and consult with your insurance provider to ensure you have appropriate earthquake coverage.

- Flood Prevention: Evaluate your property's flood risk and take measures to prevent flood damage, such as installing flood barriers, elevating electrical systems, and considering flood insurance coverage.

- Storm Preparedness: Prepare for severe weather events by trimming tree branches near your home, securing loose items in your yard, and reinforcing doors and windows.

Part 3: Home Maintenance and Upgrades

Regular home maintenance and strategic upgrades can not only prevent potential damage but also improve the overall condition and safety of your property. Consider the following:

- Roof Maintenance: Regularly inspect and maintain your roof to prevent leaks and structural damage. Replace damaged shingles and address any issues promptly.

- Plumbing Maintenance: Regularly check for plumbing leaks and address them promptly to prevent water damage and mold growth.

- Electrical System Updates: Consider updating your electrical system to meet current safety standards. Replace outdated wiring and upgrade your electrical panel if necessary.

- Home Upgrades: Certain home upgrades, such as installing impact-resistant windows, upgrading your heating and cooling systems, or improving insulation, can enhance safety, energy efficiency, and potentially lower insurance premiums.

Part 4: Risk Mitigation for Liability Claims

Liability claims can be financially and emotionally draining. Taking steps to mitigate these risks can help protect you and potentially reduce your insurance premiums:

- Dog Ownership: If you own a dog, ensure it receives proper training, socialization, and supervision to minimize the risk of dog-related liability claims.

- Property Hazards: Regularly inspect your property for potential hazards, such as uneven walkways, loose handrails, or unfenced pools. Address these hazards promptly to reduce the risk of accidents and liability claims.

- Liability Umbrella Insurance: Consider purchasing liability umbrella insurance, which provides additional liability coverage beyond the limits of your standard home insurance policy. This extra layer of protection can offer peace of mind and potentially reduce your overall insurance costs.

Conclusion

Preventative measures play a crucial role in reducing risks and potentially lowering your home insurance premiums. By implementing home safety and security measures, preparing for natural disasters, maintaining your home, and mitigating liability risks, you can create a safer environment for your property and occupants.

Remember to regularly review your insurance policy and discuss potential discounts with your insurance provider. Many insurance companies offer discounts for safety and security features, such as alarm systems or impact-resistant windows. By taking advantage of these discounts, you can potentially reduce your insurance premiums while improving the safety and security of your home.

In the upcoming chapters, we'll delve into more essential topics of home insurance, such as understanding the claims process, maintaining your home to prevent claims, and preparing for your policy renewal. By combining your knowledge of preventative measures with these topics, you'll be well-prepared to navigate the world of home insurance effectively, protect your most significant investment – your home – and enjoy the benefits of a safer and more affordable insurance experience.

THE IMPACT OF TECHNOLOGICAL ADVANCES ON HOME INSURANCE

Technological advancements have transformed various aspects of our lives, and the insurance industry is no exception. From smart home devices to data analytics, technology has brought new opportunities and challenges to the realm of home insurance. This chapter explores the impact of technological advances on home insurance and how they are reshaping the industry.

Part 1: Smart Home Devices and Monitoring Systems

Smart home devices, such as security systems, video doorbells, and connected sensors, have become increasingly popular among homeowners. These devices offer enhanced security, convenience, and energy efficiency. They also have a significant impact on home insurance:

- Risk Reduction: Smart home devices can help prevent losses and reduce risks. For instance, security systems and video surveillance cameras can deter burglars, lowering the likelihood of theft. This risk reduction may result in lower insurance premiums or potential discounts from insurers.

- Early Detection and Response: Connected sensors for smoke, water leaks, and carbon monoxide can provide early detection of potential hazards, allowing homeowners to respond quickly and mitigate damage. This early detection can help prevent small incidents from escalating into more significant claims.

- Monitoring and Notifications: Smart home devices can send real-time notifications to homeowners' smartphones, alerting them to potential issues, such as a break-in or a water leak. This instant awareness enables homeowners to take immediate action and notify their insurance providers promptly.

Part 2: Data Analytics and Telematics

Data analytics and telematics have revolutionized the insurance industry by enabling insurers to gather and analyze vast amounts of data. These technologies have specific implications for home insurance:

- Risk Assessment: Insurers can use data analytics to assess risks more accurately. By analyzing data related to a homeowner's location, property characteristics, and previous claims history, insurers can determine a more precise risk profile and tailor coverage and premiums accordingly.

- Pricing and Underwriting: Data analytics allows insurers to price policies more accurately based on the specific risks associated with a property. This can result in fairer premiums that better reflect the individual homeowner's risk profile.

- Claims Processing: Data analytics can streamline the claims process by automating various tasks, such as damage assessment and estimating repair costs. This can lead to faster and more efficient claims processing, benefiting homeowners by expediting the settlement of their claims.

Part 3: Cybersecurity and Data Privacy

As technology advances, the protection of personal data and cybersecurity becomes paramount. Home insurance policies need to address these concerns:

- Cybersecurity Coverage: With the increasing number of smart devices connected to homes, the risk of cyber threats and data breaches also rises. Home insurance policies may offer cybersecurity coverage to protect homeowners from financial losses and liabilities associated with cyber incidents.

- Data Privacy: Insurers must prioritize data privacy and ensure that homeowners' personal information collected through smart home devices is handled securely and in compliance with privacy regulations.

Part 4: Challenges and Considerations

While technological advances bring many benefits to home insurance, there are also challenges and considerations to address:

- Accessibility and Affordability: While smart home devices offer advantages, not all homeowners may have access to or be able to afford these technologies. Insurers need to ensure that their coverage remains accessible and affordable to a broad range of homeowners.

- Data Security: Insurers must invest in robust cybersecurity measures to protect the sensitive data collected from homeowners and prevent data breaches that could result in financial losses or reputational damage.

- Ethical Use of Data: Insurers should establish clear guidelines for the ethical use of data, ensuring transparency and obtaining appropriate consent from homeowners for the collection and use of their data.

Conclusion

Technological advances have transformed the home insurance industry, bringing benefits such as risk reduction, improved underwriting, faster claims processing, and enhanced security. Smart home devices and data analytics offer homeowners the opportunity to protect their properties more effectively and potentially reduce insurance premiums.

However, as technology continues to evolve, insurers must address challenges related to accessibility, affordability, data security, and ethical use of data. Striking the right balance between leveraging technology and maintaining a human-centric approach is crucial for insurers to provide comprehensive, secure, and accessible home insurance coverage.

As a homeowner, it's important to stay informed about technological advancements and how they impact home insurance. Consider adopting smart home devices that align with your needs and budget. Explore the benefits of data analytics-driven underwriting and claims processing when selecting an insurance provider. Also, be aware of data privacy and cybersecurity concerns, and ensure that your insurer takes adequate measures to protect your personal information.

In the following chapters, we'll delve into more essential topics of home insurance, such as understanding the claims process, disaster preparedness, and preparing for your policy renewal. By combining your knowledge of technological advancements with these topics, you'll be well-equipped to navigate the world of home insurance effectively and make informed decisions to protect your most significant investment – your home.

Remember that while technology can enhance home insurance, it's the combination of proactive measures, risk prevention, and comprehensive coverage that truly provides peace of mind. Embrace the benefits that technological advances bring, but always prioritize the safety and protection of your home and personal information.

CHANGING INSURANCE POLICIES: WHEN, WHY, AND HOW TO SWITCH

Insurance needs can change over time due to various factors such as life events, financial considerations, or dissatisfaction with your current insurance provider. Knowing when, why, and how to switch insurance policies is essential to ensure that you have the right coverage for your evolving needs. This chapter explores the key considerations involved in changing insurance policies.

Part 1: Evaluating Your Insurance Needs

Before making any changes to your insurance policies, it's crucial to assess your current insurance needs and determine if your existing coverage aligns with those needs. Consider the following factors:

- Life Changes: Significant life events such as getting married, having children, or purchasing a new home can impact your insurance needs. Reassess your coverage to ensure it adequately protects your assets and accounts for any new risks.

- Financial Considerations: Changes in your financial situation, such as an increase in income or the ability to save more, might prompt you to adjust your coverage levels or explore cost-saving options.

- Insurance Policy Review: Periodically review your insurance policies to understand the coverage limits, exclusions, and deductibles. Determine if any gaps exist in your coverage that should be addressed.

Part 2: Reasons to Consider Changing Insurance Policies

There are several valid reasons to consider changing insurance policies:

- Cost Considerations: If you find that your insurance premiums are continuously increasing, it may be worth shopping around for more affordable options. Request quotes from multiple insurers to compare prices while ensuring that the coverage provided meets your needs.

- Dissatisfaction with Current Provider: If you are dissatisfied with your current insurance provider due to poor customer service, claims handling, or a lack of personalized attention, it may be a sign that it's time to switch to a new provider that better aligns with your expectations.

- Changes in Coverage Needs: As your circumstances change, your coverage needs may evolve as well. For example, if you've made significant renovations to your home or acquired valuable assets, you may require increased coverage or additional policy types such as umbrella insurance.

Part 3: Switching Insurance Providers

When switching insurance providers, it's important to follow a systematic approach to ensure a smooth transition:

- Research and Comparison: Obtain quotes from multiple insurance companies to compare coverage options, pricing, and customer reviews. Consider working with an independent insurance agent who can provide unbiased advice and access to a wide range of insurers.

- Notify Your Current Provider: Before switching, inform your current insurance provider of your intention to cancel your policy. Follow their procedures for cancellation, including any required notice periods.

- Avoid Coverage Gaps: Ensure that you have new coverage in place before canceling your existing policy. This will prevent any gaps in coverage that could leave you financially exposed.

- Policy Documentation: Review the new policy carefully to understand the coverage, deductibles, limits, and exclusions. Make sure it meets your needs and addresses any concerns you had with your previous policy.

- Seamless Transition: Coordinate the start date of your new policy with the cancellation date of your current policy to ensure a seamless transition. Keep records of communication, cancellation notices, and new policy documents for reference.

Conclusion

Changing insurance policies is a significant decision that should be based on careful evaluation of your insurance needs, cost considerations, and overall satisfaction with your current provider. Regularly reviewing your policies, comparing coverage options, and staying informed about changes in your circumstances will help you make informed decisions about switching insurance providers.

In the following chapters, we'll delve into more essential topics of home insurance, such as understanding the claims process, disaster preparedness, and maintaining your home to prevent claims. By combining your knowledge of changing insurance policies with these topics, you'll be well-equipped to navigate the world of home insurance effectively and make informed decisions to protect your most significant investment – your home.

Remember, switching insurance policies should not be taken lightly. It requires careful consideration of your coverage needs, an evaluation of available options, and a thorough understanding of the terms and conditions of the new policy. Always prioritize having adequate coverage that aligns with your needs and provides the level of protection you require.

Additionally, when switching insurance providers, be sure to maintain open communication with both your current and prospective insurers. Notify your current provider of your intention to switch and follow their procedures for cancellation. At the same time, work closely with your new insurer to ensure a smooth transition and to have your new policy in effect before canceling the existing one.

While cost considerations are essential, remember that the cheapest policy may not always provide the comprehensive coverage and service you need. It's crucial to strike a balance between affordability and the quality of coverage and service offered by the insurance provider.

Lastly, consider seeking guidance from an independent insurance agent who can provide personalized advice and assist you throughout the process of changing insurance policies. Their expertise and knowledge of the insurance market can help you make informed decisions and find the right coverage at the best value.

By understanding when, why, and how to switch insurance policies, you can ensure that your coverage remains up to date, cost-effective, and aligned with your evolving needs. Take the time to evaluate your insurance needs regularly, explore available options, and make informed decisions to protect your home and assets effectively.

FUTURE TRENDS IN HOME INSURANCE: STAYING AHEAD OF THE CURVE

The world of home insurance is evolving rapidly, driven by technological advancements, changing customer expectations, and emerging risks. Staying ahead of the curve in the dynamic landscape of home insurance requires a keen understanding of future trends and their implications. This chapter explores some of the key trends shaping the future of home insurance and provides insights on how homeowners can adapt to these changes.

Part 1: Technology-Driven Advancements

- Internet of Things (IoT): The proliferation of smart home devices and IoT technology allows for greater connectivity and data collection. Insurers can leverage IoT to offer more personalized coverage, monitor risks, and provide real-time assistance to homeowners.

- Telematics and Usage-Based Insurance: Telematics, commonly used in auto insurance, is expanding to home insurance. By using sensors and data analytics, insurers can assess risk in real-time, customize coverage based on usage patterns, and incentivize policyholders with lower premiums for responsible behavior.

- Artificial Intelligence (AI) and Data Analytics: AI and data analytics are transforming various aspects of insurance, including underwriting, claims processing, and risk assessment. Insurers can leverage AI algorithms to analyze vast amounts of data, identify patterns, and make data-driven decisions, leading to more accurate risk assessment and efficient claims handling.

Part 2: Personalization and Customization

- Tailored Coverage Options: Increasingly, insurers are offering personalized coverage options that cater to individual homeowners' unique needs. This includes coverage for specific possessions, customization based on lifestyle factors, and flexible policy terms.

- Parametric Insurance: Parametric insurance, based on predetermined triggers rather than traditional claims processes, provides coverage for specific risks such as natural disasters. It offers quicker claims settlements and greater transparency, making it an attractive option for homeowners in high-risk areas.

Part 3: Climate Change and Environmental Considerations

- Risk Assessment and Mitigation: As climate change brings about more frequent and severe weather events, insurers are investing in improved risk assessment models and partnering with homeowners to mitigate risks. This may involve providing incentives for sustainable home features or offering guidance on disaster preparedness.

- Parametric and Index-Based Insurance: Parametric and index-based insurance products are gaining traction in regions vulnerable to climate-related risks. These products provide coverage based on predefined weather parameters, allowing for quicker claims payouts and reducing the administrative burden on homeowners.

Part 4: Digital Transformation and Customer Experience

- Digital Self-Service: Insurers are investing in user-friendly digital platforms, allowing homeowners to manage their policies, file claims, and access information conveniently. These self-service capabilities enhance the overall customer experience and streamline insurance processes.

- Virtual Claims Handling: Virtual claims handling, including remote inspections and digital documentation, is becoming more prevalent. By leveraging technologies like video calls and image recognition, insurers can expedite the claims process, reduce costs, and improve customer satisfaction.

Part 5: Risk Prevention and Loss Mitigation

- Preventative Technologies: Insurers are increasingly focusing on proactive risk prevention through technologies such as smart sensors, leak detection systems, and home monitoring. Homeowners who adopt these technologies may qualify for lower premiums or discounts.

- Collaboration and Education: Insurers are working closely with homeowners to educate them on risk prevention strategies and provide guidance on home maintenance. By promoting proactive measures, insurers aim to reduce claims frequency and severity.

Conclusion

The future of home insurance is being shaped by technological advancements, evolving customer expectations, and emerging risks. As a homeowner, staying ahead of the curve requires a proactive approach to understanding these trends and adapting to the changing landscape of home insurance.

To stay ahead of the curve, consider the following strategies:

- Stay Informed: Continuously educate yourself about emerging trends and advancements in home insurance. Follow industry news, attend seminars or webinars, and engage with experts to stay updated on the latest developments.

- Evaluate Your Coverage: Regularly review your insurance coverage to ensure it aligns with your evolving needs. Consider if new technologies, such as smart home devices or parametric insurance, can provide added value or better protection for your home and assets.

- Embrace Technology: Embrace technology-driven advancements in home insurance. Explore the potential benefits of IoT devices, telematics, and digital self-service platforms offered by insurers. Assess how these technologies can improve your insurance experience and help you better manage risks.

- Engage with Insurers: Stay connected with your insurance provider to understand the innovative offerings they have or plan to introduce. Engage in discussions about new coverage options, risk prevention strategies, and ways to optimize your policy to suit your needs.

- Consider Sustainable Practices: As climate change becomes a significant concern, consider adopting sustainable practices within your home. Install energy-efficient features, reinforce your home against weather-related risks, and explore insurance products that incentivize and reward environmentally friendly behaviors.

- Seek Expert Advice: Consult with independent insurance agents or experts who have in-depth knowledge of the evolving home insurance landscape. They can provide personalized guidance, help you navigate through new insurance options, and assist in finding the best coverage for your specific needs.

- Maintain Open Communication: Establish open lines of communication with your insurance provider. Regularly discuss your changing needs, ask questions about emerging trends, and inquire about available discounts or policy enhancements. Building a strong relationship with your insurer can ensure you receive the most relevant and beneficial coverage options.

By actively engaging with the future trends in home insurance and adapting to the changing landscape, you can stay ahead of the curve and make informed decisions about your coverage. Embrace technology, evaluate your needs regularly, and collaborate with your insurance provider to optimize your policy and protect your home and assets effectively.

In conclusion, the future of home insurance is driven by technological advancements, personalized coverage options, environmental considerations, and a focus on risk prevention. By staying informed, embracing innovation, and maintaining a proactive approach, you can navigate the evolving home insurance landscape with confidence and ensure that your coverage remains relevant, effective, and tailored to your unique needs.

www.ingramcontent.com/pod-product-compliance
Lightning Source LLC
Chambersburg PA
CBHW070654220526
45466CB00001B/437